UNCOMMON
ACCELERATION

UNCOMMON ACCELERATION

*DISCOVERING HOW TO ENGAGE
WITH SPIRITUAL LAWS THAT
TRANSCEND NATURAL LIMITATIONS*

DR. ARPITHA KOMANAPALLI

Dedication

There is something to be said about the miraculous discovery of how to engage with the spiritual laws that transcend natural limitations. You have the potential to experience God's supernatural power in your life, and to see results that go beyond what you thought possible.

I want to dedicate this book and share my heartfelt gratitude to my husband, Pastor Benjamin Komanapalli Jr., whose teachings and unwavering faith have profoundly impacted my life and ministry. His support and guidance have been instrumental in the creation of this book.

Foreword

Uncommon Acceleration unveils profound spiritual principles that serve as catalysts for extraordinary success. Through compelling personal narratives, Dr. Arpitha Komanapalli illustrates how unwavering faith in God can unlock transformative breakthroughs that transcend mere human potential.

This work beckons you to awaken to your divine potential and embrace the extraordinary opportunities that await. With steadfast faith, the realm of remarkable achievements lies just beyond the horizon.

Apostle Grace Lubega
Phaneroo Ministrie

Contents

Prologue

When I look around and see so many hardworking individuals striving to achieve their dreams but falling short of the extraordinary outcomes they desire, I feel a deep calling to share what I have learned in my walk of faith. This book, "Uncommon Acceleration", is born out of a desire to help you unlock the spiritual principles that can transform your efforts into supernatural results.

One of the most significant influences on this book is the incredible growth of our church. We began in a small, confined room, but through faith and divine intervention, we experienced an acceleration that was nothing short of miraculous. This journey has been a powerful testament to me of what God can do when we align ourselves with His Word and purposes. The central message of this book is simple yet profound: **Believe in God and trust His Word**.

When you place your faith in Him, you open the door to uncommon results and miraculous breakthroughs.

Before you dive into this book, I want you to be aware of a few key concepts. The spiritual laws I discuss here are rooted in a deep belief in God and a steadfast trust in His promises. As you embrace these truths, you will begin to see the supernatural at work in your life. My prayer is that you will grow in your faith and trust in the God who can do the impossible. May you experience His power in your life and see the uncommon results that only He can bring.

With faith and hope,
Dr. Arpitha Komanapalli

1

What is Uncommon Acceleration?

"But as it is written: 'Eye has not seen, nor ear heard, nor have entered into the heart of man the things which God has prepared for those who love Him.'"

I Corinthians 2:9 (NKJV)

What does it look like when God intervenes in your life; when He steps into your situation and does what only He can do? The impossible is made possible through His grace and power. Whether it's health struggles, financial difficulties, a troubled marriage, or a failing business: No matter what you're going through, when God steps in, He completely turns it around for your good. There is sudden restoration, healing, provision, and favor in your life.

Every difficult circumstance becomes marked by His unparalleled grace and power, as He accelerates His plans and blessings for you. This is Uncommon Acceleration.

Uncommon Acceleration is when God intervenes and orchestrates extraordinary changes with divine speed. It's when He brings about a net-breaking, boat-sinking, overflowing and beyond imagination kind of breakthrough. It's as if the barriers holding you back are suddenly removed, and you find yourself living the abundant life that is promised to you.

In this book, we will look at how God can accelerate progress in your life beyond what you thought possible. By understanding and believing in this divine quickening, you can witness miracles and breakthroughs occurring faster than you ever imagined. Prepare to experience the amazing power of God's acceleration in your life.

What Does Uncommon Acceleration Look Like?

Uncommon acceleration happens when God steps in. It is a divine quickening and supernatural advancement that takes place in your life. God intervenes in your situation and brings kingdom solutions. In His sovereignty, He has the power to accelerate His plans, promises and blessings over you in such a way that is beyond your understanding.

Perhaps you were jobless the last few months, and now, all of a sudden, you have miraculously secured a high-paying position. Or maybe you struggled to conceive for years, and now you are expecting a child. You sought prayer to save your marriage from divorce, but now you and your spouse are praying together. You considered shutting down your business, but now you manage three thriving enterprises. Doctors once insisted on chemo or surgery, yet here you are, completely made whole. In a family accustomed to taking loans, you've managed to acquire a debt-free home.

These are the kind of testimonies that will emerge when you believe for Uncommon Acceleration in your life! Goals are achieved, opportunities are opened up, and dreams are made manifest. For some of you, uncommon acceleration might be so swift that by the time you finish reading this book, you will have already experienced a breakthrough without even anticipating it. This is because faith is rising within you as you read the Word of God.

The Principle of Sowing and Reaping

In the principle of 'sowing and reaping', the process looks something like this: You sow the seed, you wait a while, and you receive a harvest. There is always a sequence of interconnected stages that must happen before we receive the final results.

SEED → TIME → HARVEST

However, in the season of uncommon acceleration, we see something incredible takes place. God steps in and brings divine acceleration! The process now looks something like this:

SEED → (TIME) HARVEST

True! The principle of sowing and reaping remains, but our God is a sovereign God and the laws and principles of nature and time bend their knees before Him. He stands outside of time and is not bound by it. The very concept of time was created for mankind, and it is in His power to compress time or stretch it for us. In uncommon acceleration, you sow, and you reap. That is, you simply believe and receive.

You are Chosen

Let us look at David and how he made a mark in his time. Among the many stones by the riverside, David chose five. And from the five stones that he carried in his pocket, he picked out one. That stone was 'set apart' from the other four stones. It was that stone that struck the head of the giant. The others could not because they lacked the necessary momentum. In the right person's hand, an ordinary pebble was transformed into a giant-slaying weapon. You might feel like a small stone—insignificant. However, when you are in the hands of God in the season of acceleration, you will accomplish the purpose for which you were created.

Perhaps you think these kinds of miracles and extraordinary things happen only to a chosen few. You might even think, "I don't need those things to happen in my life. All I need is my breakthrough." The fear of dreaming big and facing disappointment may hold you back. But let me encourage you with this: the Word of God says that you are chosen. You are uniquely created, and there's nobody else like you. Even though there are 8 billion people on this planet, God will make room for your dreams!

He has given you divine vision for a reason. There is a great purpose attached to your life. He affirms you and values you. Moreover, there is no one else quite like you in this world; you are unique and precious to Him. The things God will do in and through you are going to be so exceptional that people around you will be amazed. So, do not fear to dream big. Trust in God's unique plan for you and hold fast to your confession, believing that His extraordinary promises will manifest in your life.

I Corinthians 2:9 (NIV) says, *"What no eye has seen, what no ear has heard, and what no human mind has conceived.*" Such are the things that God has prepared for you. Like David's stone, you are set apart. He has placed a distinct calling on your life. You are called to do and accomplish unique things. Consider the instance of Jesus restoring sight to the blind man (Matthew 20, Mark 8, and John 9); until that point, many prophets in the Old Testament had performed mighty miracles, but none had opened blind eyes. This shows us the reality of what God is able and willing to do. Even if something was never done before, you can still believe for it to happen in your life. This is what the Bible means by '*what no eye has seen, what no ear has heard*' (1 Corinthians 2:9-10). Similarly, in the book of Acts, we see the apostles walking in that distinctive anointing, performing unusual and uncommon miracles. Even their shadows and handkerchiefs used by them were ministering healing to people.

When we read the words '*No eye has seen and no ear has heard,*' it's important to understand that these miracles, though astonishing, have already been seen and heard. Yet, the things that God has in store for us, the things He has called us to do, are even greater than those performed by the prophets of the old testament or the apostles of the new testament.

As you respond to God's calling and stay connected to the Word of God, you will begin to tap into supernatural grace and favor. Just as these uncommon miracles happened in the pages of scripture, so shall they happen in your own life. Have faith in the limitless potential of God and accept this truth.

Examples of Uncommon Acceleration

The concept of uncommon acceleration can be illustrated through the analogy of a bamboo tree. The first step is to plant the seed in the soil. You then water it diligently, fertilize it daily and nurture it with care—repeating the process day after day for an entire year. Nothing seems to be emerging from the ground. The second and third years pass by with no visible growth. The fourth year also goes by with little indication of progress. However, in the fifth year, slowly and surely, you will begin to see something sprouting. Once it does, you will see that the little bamboo sapling grows two inches every hour!

This means it will grow four feet in 24 hours! Just a day ago, you saw nothing, but today it stands four feet tall! And it doesn't stop there. The bamboo tree continues to grow at this rapid pace, eventually reaching about 90 feet in height. The bamboo tree remains underground for what feels like a long time. Similarly, you may feel unseen, unheard, or unnoticed. At the surface level, it may seem as though you are not making any progress. Everything you try to do may seem to amount to nothing. But know this: your roots are growing deeper and deeper to sustain the growth that is about to come. You are being prepared for great acceleration.

For the kind of anointing, blessing, and fruit that will emerge from your life, it is essential that your roots be deep and your foundation be strong. In the season of uncommon acceleration, much like the bamboo tree, once you begin to rise, you'll grow at a rapid pace. Such growth cannot be ignored, as it comes from God through grace. It is a testament to the goodness of God.

So shall it be in your life—every hour, every day, inch by inch, strength to strength, glory to glory, blessing upon blessing. Testimonies will keep flowing in. You will experience supernatural miracles from God. This is the acceleration God is going to bring to you!

If we observe a long jumper in the Olympics, with a single leap, he aims to achieve the longest forward jump. However, just before he takes that leap, he performs an action that seems contrary to his goal. He takes a few steps backward! He steps backwards in order to gain momentum and build acceleration.

This principle is evident in many areas. In archery, an arrow must be first pulled back before it can be released to hit its target. If you want to force open a door that is shut tight, step back, use momentum and push it open. Through acceleration, the doors that have been previously shut in your life, can now be forced open.

Perhaps over the past few weeks, months, or even years, you may have felt as though you are moving backward. Just like the long jumper who steps back to gain momentum for his leap or the archer who pulls back the arrow before releasing it to hit the target, these moments of seeming regression are actually preparing you for a powerful acceleration. The Holy Spirit is helping you build up speed for that long jump He has been preparing you for. Remember, the doors in your life that are opened through this acceleration can never be shut again. Embrace this period of preparation, knowing that God is setting you up for an extraordinary leap forward.

Through this book, it is my prayer that you will take hold of this revelation and begin to walk in its fullness. I cannot define what acceleration will look like for you. However, I encourage you to seek God and ask Him to reveal the areas in your life where He is bringing acceleration. Ask Him to give you vision for what He wants to do in you. When He reveals it to you, hold on to His word and claim His promises.

Reflections

- Recount a time God has intervened in your life and brought miraculous breakthroughs in different seasons. Acknowledge His hand over you and thank Him for the wondrous things He has done.

- There is great purpose attached to your life. He affirms you: He values you. There is no one else quite like you in this world. You are unique and precious to Him. Spend a few moments reflecting on these words and receive the affirmation and God's love for you.

- Note down the areas in which you need to see "Uncommon Acceleration" and seek the Lord for clarity, direction, and discernment.

2

Prepare for Manifestation

"Do you not know that those who run in a race all run, but one receives the prize? Run in such a way that you may obtain it."

I Corinthians 9:24 (NKJV)

It All Starts With Grace

Uncommon acceleration is possible only through the grace of God. Whether it is the swift growth of your business, the sudden breakthrough in your marriage, or the supernatural healing in your body—all of these are the manifestations of God's grace working in your life. It takes maturity to understand that growth comes because of grace.

Yes, you are the one performing the tasks and putting in the hard work. However, it is crucial to recognize that true increase comes from God alone. He alone is our source. As you persevere, God will propel you towards your destiny in a way that only He can.

Grace vs. Effort

Let us examine the distinction between grace and effort. God's grace is not an excuse for laziness. The gift of grace does not absolve us from responsibility or exempt us from hard work. We must, in fact, work from a place of grace.

In I Corinthians 15:10 (ESV), Paul explains, *"But by the grace of God I am what I am, and his grace toward me was not in vain. On the contrary, I worked harder than any of them, though it was not I, but the grace of God that is with me."* People may think, "Oh, I don't have to do anything, but just receive the grace of God!" However, the grace of God doesn't make one lazy or encourage laziness. In fact, God provides grace to accomplish the things that He has asked you to do.

It is simple: God's grace meets our human capacity and expands it. We suddenly find ourselves able to accomplish things we previously could not in our own strength. His grace enables us to work with ease, but it is not without effort. It involves deliberate focus and investment of time in the things of God. It requires addressing the internal issues of our hearts. It requires us to run in such a way as to obtain the prize. (1 Corinthians 9:24). It involves disciplining our character and training ourselves. We must train our mind to think in line with heaven, align our attitudes to reflect the Word of God and do all our work as unto the Lord.

Self-Reliance vs. Trust

We also need to train our minds to trust God more than ourselves. Self-reliance is to trust in yourself, which means you exclude God from all your decisions. When we have a mindset of self-reliance, we prioritize our plans over God's purpose for us. We will be driven by our personal ambitions rather than seek God's direction.

Can the bamboo tree grow on its own? On the outside, it may appear rigid and resilient, but it still needs to depend on external factors for growth and sustenance. We must recognise that God is our source. He is the ultimate source of wisdom, power, strength and provision. There is only so much you can achieve through your own ability.

Stepping into divine acceleration will

require complete surrender to the move of God. It demands that you live in such a way that you are utterly dependent on Him. Yes, you might feel as though you are losing control. Yes, you may feel as though you have lost a sense of security. Yes, you might think that you're not making significant progress outwardly. But if God has set a destiny for your life, it will certainly take His involvement to fulfill it.

As challenging as this might seem to be, rely on the Holy Spirit and surrender all self-reliance. Allow God to increase your dependency on Him day by day. Trust in the Lord with all your heart and lean not on your own understanding, and He will direct your path. (Proverbs 3:5-6).

The Unseen Realm

You must also know that whatever

happens in the earthly realm must first take place in the spiritual realm. It all starts there—in the unseen world. This means that you cannot move physically if you do not move spiritually. It is "on earth as it is in Heaven."

As the sons and daughters of God, we have the authority to tap into the heavens and claim the things of the Spirit for ourselves and our families. We need to speak what heaven speaks. Unless you understand spiritual principles, you won't be able to experience uncommon acceleration.

"It is the spirit that quickeneth; the flesh profiteth nothing..."

John 6:63 *(KJV)*

What is quickening things in your life? It is the Holy Spirit. Allow the Holy Spirit to breathe over everything you do.

There is Purpose Behind your Breakthrough

Paul says in I Corinthians 9:26 (NIV), *"Therefore I do not run like someone running aimlessly; I do not fight like a boxer beating the air."* You are not running without direction or putting in efforts aimlessly. There is a reason for this uncommon acceleration in your life. In your growing and in your pressing forward, there is great purpose in the kingdom of God.

Consider this scenario: Suppose you attend a series of prayer meetings. Here, you encounter God and experience a total transformation. Your mind is renewed and your hope is restored. You have believed God for provision, and by His grace, you have secured a job. Now comes the challenge. Will you continue to remain faithful and pursue the things of God? Or will you abuse God's grace and become complacent in your spiritual walk? Will you still devote time to prayer meetings now that you have received your blessing?

Remember and recognize that it was the grace of God that helped you achieve your goals in the first place. You have to find ways to prioritize God's presence in both the valley and the mountaintop. Serve Him when you're waiting for a miracle, as well as when you have received your reward.   Let your breakthrough be the reason for you to become a blessing in the Kingdom. Perhaps you can now choose to be present at the prayer meeting half an hour early to serve or, now that God has brought financial increase, decide to not only continue giving your tithe but even give twice or thrice as much unto the Lord.

As God's grace accelerates your progress,

learn to channel your time, energy, and dedication toward His Kingdom. Don't lose sight of the purpose behind your breakthrough. Before acceleration arrives, ensure you are deeply rooted in this understanding. And when acceleration does come, stay the course!

Reflections

- Reflect on the "why" behind your breakthrough. Open your heart to God and allow your intentions to be in line with His.

- On a scale of 1-10, how do you rate yourself in a place of surrender to God?

- Is your breakthrough holding you back or encouraging you to invest time in building God's kingdom? Align your priorities to ensure you remain committed to serving Him and His Church.

3

Activating Uncommon Acceleration

"Therefore we also, since we are surrounded by so great a cloud of witnesses, let us lay aside every weight, and the sin which so easily ensnares us, and let us run with endurance the race that is set before us."

Hebrews 12:1-2 (NKJV)

The Things that Hold Us Back

In the scripture quoted above, Paul urges us to run with perseverance. He emphasizes the importance of laying aside any burdens we might be carrying. If a runner holds onto weights while running, it will slow their pace. You must set aside these weights to run swiftly. Weights will only serve as setbacks in your spiritual journey. The Bible equates weight with sin. While none of us are exempt from temptation and we all stumble occasionally, God invites us back into His presence.

When we believe in Jesus and claim His blood over us, we are made righteous and our sins are washed away. Paul, in I Corinthians 10:23 (NKJV) says, *"All things are lawful for me, but not all things are helpful; all things are lawful for me, but not all things edify."* As Paul says, not everything is beneficial. We are free to do anything, but not everything is beneficial, and will help us reach our destiny. We need to develop such maturity to discern the things that will weigh us down and hinder our spiritual growth.

People often ask whether activities like watching movies or socializing in pubs are morally objectionable. While such activities are permissible, they have the potential to become burdensome, leading to a deceleration in your pursuit. Anything that keeps you away from walking in the fullness of what God has for you is not worth it. It will only slow you down from reaching your divine destiny and leave you in a state of spiritual stagnation.

We must learn to identify and let go of the 'weights' that we carry in our day-to-day lives. Remember, anger is a weight; so is unforgiveness.

Family disputes and workplace stress can also be weights. The enemy is aware of the impact that uncommon acceleration will bring and will attempt to distract, disrupt, and delay your progress. Do not yield to these distractions. Unnecessary conflicts with your spouse, frustration towards your neighbor, and job-related stress are all burdens that can impede your acceleration.

While you're believing for divine acceleration, you have the potential to grow at two inches per hour—equivalent to four feet per day. Why would you want to add unnecessary weight? Why would you limit your growth? Choose to let go of every unnecessary weight and declare over yourself, "I'm advancing at God's pace, and I refuse to let these burdens slow me down." Amen.

Reuben and the Twelve Tribes

Let us learn from the twelve tribes of Israel. Reuben was the firstborn of Israel. He had the birthright benefits of the firstborn. He carried three anointings: the anointing of the firstborn, the kingly anointing, and the priestly anointing. The name of Reuben should have been written and appeared frequently on multiple pages of the Bible. However, despite being anointed, he placed a heavy weight on his own growth; as a result, his name gradually faded from the Biblical narrative. By defiling his father's bed, he disregarded his calling. Consequently, the birthright passed to Joseph, the kingly anointing to Judah, and the priestly anointing to Levi.

Even though Joseph was the second youngest, he walked with vision and integrity. He chose to cast aside every weight that so easily ensnares. Like Reuben, Joseph also faced different opportunities to give into sin in secret —opportunities that no one would have known about. Yet, unlike his brother, he did not yield to sin. In the spiritual realm, everything is accounted for, and every action is recorded.

As a result, although the tribes of Israel do not include a tribe of Joseph, his sons, Manasseh and Ephraim, became tribes of their own. Joseph's sons reached the status of brothers, while Joseph himself was elevated to a patriarchal position. This illustrates the profound acceleration in Joseph's life: he went from being the second youngest among his brothers to transitioning into a fatherly role, skipping a generation. Nothing on this earth can accomplish this except the grace of God. This is Uncommon Acceleration.

We must ask ourselves: Are there activities or habits hindering my progress or causing stagnation in my journey? Am I prioritizing the things that bring me closer to God and help me fulfill my purpose? Lean in to the help of the Holy Spirit, who is ever available, and able to sanctify you.

Three Essential Steps To Activate Uncommon Acceleration

1. *Sanctify Yourself*

Sanctification is the primary step to activate acceleration. It is the act of dedicating oneself to seeking God and becoming more Christ-like, all the while rejecting sin and not conforming to the patterns of the world. It means to separate, set apart, consecrate, dedicate and lay aside everything that's going against the Word of God. It requires dying to yourself by laying aside every weight: the arguments, the pressures and the pleasures. All of these weights are holding back your acceleration. Remember, your aim is 90 feet, do not stop at 4 feet. Sanctified life is an open door to Uncommon Acceleration.

2. A Heart of Humility

James 4:6 (NKJV) says, *"God gives grace to the humble."* Grace brings acceleration to your life, but humility positions you to receive that grace. In other words, greatness comes through grace, and grace comes through a humble spirit. One of the characteristics of humility is to be teachable. A recent example of this is when pastor Ben heard this word and understood "Uncommon Acceleration", he received it for himself. He has surely read the Bible much more than I have, but the mark of humility is to be teachable. So even though he knows more than me, when he heard this word, in his humility he accepted it for himself and acted on it. And we as a church have experienced the fruit of his humility and obedience.

Oftentimes, without conscious knowledge, we can allow a sense of familiarity to creep into our hearts. A familiarity towards scripture, prayer forms, or even each other. This can keep us from freely receiving the wealth of revelation that God wants to release to us. For example, if we hear a topic being preached that we have already heard before, we might dismiss it without fully grabbing hold of that revelation and truly applying that word in our lives. We can easily develop a critical or judgmental heart, which does not attract the grace of God. Become moldable and remain humble. An abundance of grace awaits you.

3. Build a Prayer Life

The prayer life that you build will cause an increase in your life. If you don't move spiritually, you can't move physically. Prayer is the time you are connecting to the spiritual realm. Prayer is the time you are connecting with God. Prayer is what will bring acceleration into your life. Prayer is not playing; it is a serious, intimate time when God speaks to you.

The acceleration is coming, but I cannot describe it in detail—only God can. I pray that God will show you where you are going. I pray that God will give you the vision to know what you need to do and what your next steps are, so you can see where you are going with this uncommon acceleration. I pray you all have vision. Even with the anointing, it is sometimes not enough if you don't have the vision.

Building a strong prayer life is not just about asking for things; it's about listening and receiving direction from God. It's in these quiet moments of connection that God reveals His plans and purposes for your life. This vision will guide you through periods of acceleration and ensure that you are prepared for the blessings and challenges that come your way.

As you build your prayer life, make it a priority to seek God's vision for your life. Ask Him to show you the steps you need to take and the path you need to follow. With vision, your anointing and efforts will be focused and effective, leading to a life of purpose and fulfillment.

The Importance of Vision

In Judges 16, we see the life of Samson. After everything that Samson went through, his hair grows back, symbolizing the return of his strength and anointing. Even though he had the anointing, he lacked vision. This shows us that vision is crucial. Without it, even the most powerful anointing can be rendered ineffective.

Vision is the roadmap that guides you in your spiritual journey. It is through prayer that we receive this vision. Without vision, you might have the strength and the anointing, but you won't know where to direct them. Prayer helps you to align your actions with God's plan, ensuring that you are moving in the right direction. As you commit to building your prayer life, you will see acceleration and increase in every area of your life.

Reflections

- Spend 15 minutes praying in tongues and honor the presence of the Holy Spirit.

- Introspect your life and ask the Holy Spirit to reveal any "weights" you may be carrying. Choose to lay them all down at the feet of Jesus.

- Pray a scripture of sanctification over yourself today.

4

Faith for Uncommon Acceleration

"Yet he did not waver through unbelief regarding the promise of God, but was strengthened in his faith and gave glory to God, being fully persuaded that God had power to do what he had promised."

Romans 4:21-22 (NKJV)

The Foundation of Faith

In the construction of tall buildings, more time is often spent digging the foundation than erecting the structure itself. Once the pillars are up and the first slab is in place, the process becomes significantly smoother. This analogy underscores the importance of a solid foundation. As we prepare to enter a season of uncommon acceleration, it's crucial to establish a strong base to reach unprecedented heights in our lives. Just as buildings with weak foundations are prone to collapse, our success depends on the strength of our faith.

In our spiritual lives, a strong foundation is essential before we can experience uncommon acceleration. Faith is the bedrock of spiritual growth and progress. Just as the pillars and slabs provide stability to a building, faith provides the stability we need to withstand challenges. A well-grounded faith helps us endure the trials and tribulations we face, preventing us from collapsing under pressure.

The Bible says in Romans 4:20-21 (NIV), *"Yet he did not waver through unbelief regarding the promise of God, but was strengthened in his faith and gave glory to God, being fully persuaded that God had power to do what he had promised."* This passage offers a powerful example of holding on to God's promise through the story of Abraham, who, despite his old age and physical limitations, did not waver in his belief. He was fully persuaded that what God had promised, He was also able to perform. Faith, therefore, is about being fully convinced of God's promises, even when they are not immediately visible.

This principle of unwavering faith is also evident in the life of Paul. In Acts 27, Paul is aboard a ship caught in a violent storm. Despite the perilous situation, Paul says in Acts 27:22 (NIV), *"But now I urge you to keep up your courage, because not one of you will be lost; only the ship will be destroyed."* Paul remains confident because he believes in God's Word. He assures the others on the ship that no lives will be lost, demonstrating his steadfast faith. Faith involves holding onto God's promises regardless of our circumstances, trusting that His Word is true and will come to pass.

Growing Our Faith and
Changing Our Perspective

Faith is not static; it grows as we engage with and receive the Word of God. In Romans 12:3 (NKJV) Paul says, *"For I say, through the grace given to me, to everyone who is among you, not to think of himself more highly than he ought to think, but to think soberly, as God has dealt to each one a measure of faith."* This reminds us that God has given each one of us a measure of faith, which can increase as we immerse ourselves in God's Word. Just as the roots of a bamboo tree spread deep into the ground, our faith grows stronger and more expansive through hearing, meditating and confessing the word consistently.

This journey of faith can be visualized through various levels. Starting at Level 1, where one receives a measure of faith upon being born again, believers can ascend to higher levels as

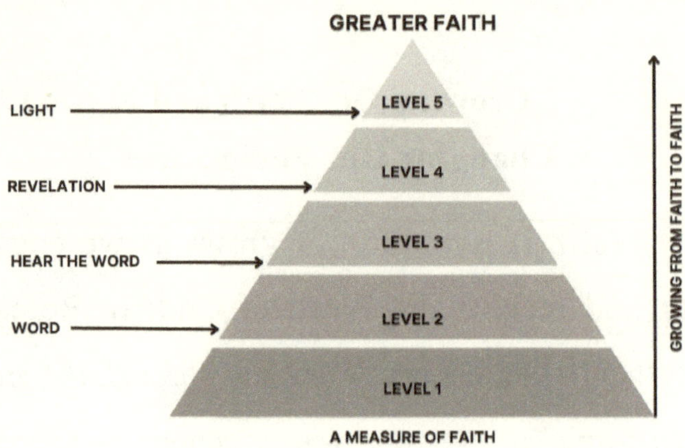

they engage more deeply with the Word of God. When they receive the word they move to the next level. And as they hear the Word and receive revelation, their faith grows and they move to the next level. Each level represents a deeper understanding and greater faith, culminating in Level 5, where the light of the Word fully illuminates their spiritual journey. As believers immerse themselves in God's Word and receive its revelations, their faith continually increases, enabling them to live more fully in alignment with God's promises.

As faith grows, perspectives change. The higher one goes spiritually, the broader their vision becomes. Just as standing on a mountain provides a wider view than standing on the ground, spiritual elevation allows for greater understanding of God's promises and provisions. Increased faith leads to greater spiritual insight, enabling believers to see the fullness of God's promises in the scriptures and understand their application in their lives.

Consider how different perspectives change with elevation. Standing on the ground, one might see only the gates of a hall. From the terrace of the hall, the entire vicinity is visible. From a mountain, parts of the city come into view. A flight reveals the entirety of the city, while a rocket provides a view of the entire planet Earth. The eyes remain the same; it is the scope of sight that changes. Similarly, ascending in the spiritual realm allows one to see what others cannot. As faith grows, God reveals greater things.

Deuteronomy 34:1 states, *"Moses went up from the plains of Moab to the top of Pisgah, opposite Jericho."* From there, Moses saw the promised land, and God showed him everything from that vantage point. Today, as one's faith grows, God can reveal the promises of the scriptures as He did for Moses. The promised land represents the provisions of the scriptures. As one ascends up in faith, the entirety of scripture becomes clear from the old covenant in Genesis to Malachi and the new covenant Matthew to Revelation—God's provision is unveiled.

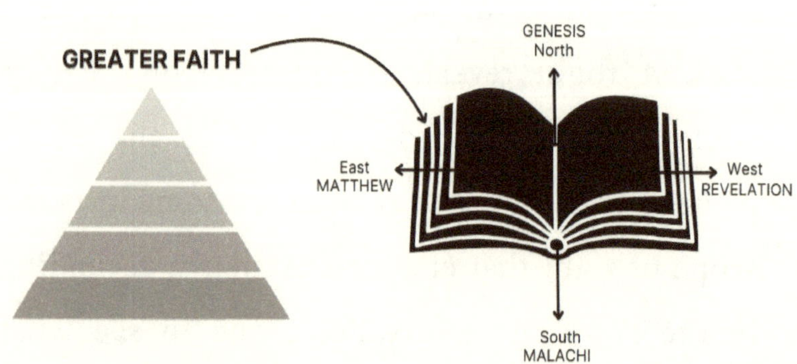

Hearing and meditating on the Word is a means of changing spiritual heights and increasing your level of faith. Spiritually ascending makes previously insurmountable problems appear smaller. Just as ascending in an airplane makes large buildings appear tiny, rising in the spiritual realm diminishes the size of one's problems. The challenges that seemed like mountains become insignificant from God's perspective. As faith increases, the perception of problems changes, and their true, smaller nature is revealed.

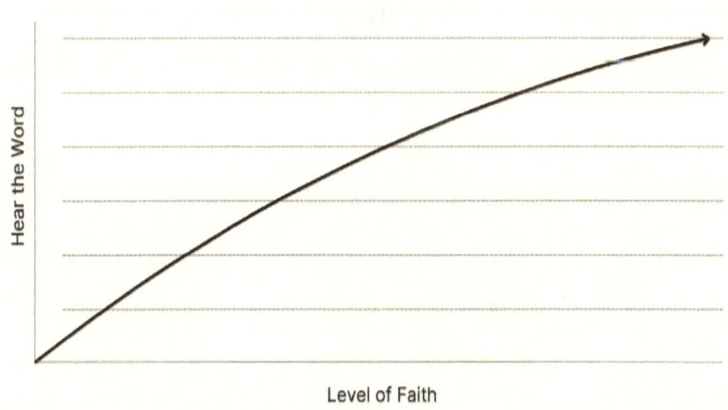

In prayers, rather than asking God to perform tasks, it is more effective to ask Him to show the way. From higher spiritual heights, God reveals the path and the true scale of situations. Revelation 4:1 says, "Come up here, I will show you things." God calls believers to higher levels of faith to reveal His perspective. This spiritual growth is achieved by hearing and immersing in the Word of God.

Embrace this season of uncommon acceleration, knowing that with faith, you can achieve the impossible and see God's promises manifest in your life. Like the bamboo tree, faith requires nurturing, patience, and perseverance to flourish and reach its full potential.

Reflections

- Reflect on the level of faith you possess at this moment. Are you fully convinced of God's promises, or do you find yourself wavering? If your faith is dwindling, ask God to increase it.

- Consider the moment you accepted Christ and were born again. When did it happen? Reflect on that transformative experience and praise God for what He has done in your life.

- Take time to read Hebrews 11. Allow the stories of faith to speak to you in a new way, inspiring and strengthening your own journey of faith.

5

Faith Comes by Hearing

"So then faith comes by hearing,
and hearing by the word of God."
Romans 10:17 (NKJV)

The Simplicity of Faith

In 1 Corinthians 1:26-27, Paul writes, *"For you see your calling, brethren, that not many wise men after the flesh, not many mighty, not many noble are called. But God has chosen the foolish things of the world to confound the wise, and God has chosen the weak things of the world to confound the things which are mighty."* This passage reminds us that faith is accessible to everyone. It doesn't require high intelligence or extensive education. You don't have to be smart to have faith. This is an important truth to embrace: faith is for everyone, regardless of their background or intellect.

God has a unique plan for each of our lives, a plan designed even before the foundations of the earth. However, the devil also has plans—schemes to instill fear, doubt, and reliance on our natural senses. His goal is to derail God's purpose for us. Despite these schemes, God's plan prevails. He doesn't need a backup plan because His first plan always works, and that plan is rooted in faith.

God has given us the strategy of faith to navigate our lives. Romans 12:3 tells us that He has distributed a measure of faith to each of us. Mark 11:22 further reveals that this faith is not just any faith, but the faith of God. In other words, God has implanted His own faith within us. Additionally, Hebrews 12:2 identifies Jesus as the author and finisher of our faith, meaning the faith within us originates from and is perfected by Him.

Hebrews 11:3 demonstrates that God Himself used this faith to create the worlds: *"Through faith we understand that the worlds were framed by the word of God."* This divine faith is powerful and creative, and God desires for us to use it in the same way He does. The world itself was shaped by God's faith, and we are called to make use of this faith in our own lives.

Understanding the origin and simplicity of faith naturally leads us to a fundamental principle: **"Faith comes by hearing, and hearing by the words of Christ."** This principle underscores the importance of immersing ourselves in the Word of God. The more we hear and receive God's Word, the stronger our faith becomes. This process is essential for spiritual growth and for navigating the challenges and opportunities we encounter. As we delve deeper into this truth, we will explore how hearing the Word of God not only strengthens our faith but also transforms our perspective and empowers us to live out God's plan for our lives.

Faith in Action

God created the earth with faith, and now we are getting ready to use our faith. Even Jesus, when He walked on the planet, showed us how to use faith. Let's consider the story of Jairus. When Jesus arrived, Jairus's daughter was already dead. But what did Jesus tell them? He said she was sleeping, and everyone laughed because they didn't understand what He was doing. Jesus, however, didn't laugh because He knew what He was going to do; He was operating on a higher level of truth.

This higher level of truth is a revelation of God. Jesus said, *"I only say what my Father says. I only do what He says to do."* So, He went to Jairus's daughter and said, *"talitha kumi"* which means, *"Arise."* He commanded her to arise now, not later. Here, Jesus was not operating linearly. He wasn't waiting for something to happen because He knew in the spiritual realm, it had already happened. In that moment, He went vertically upwards. He accessed a realm where things are already established and brought the invisible realm into the visible realm that we can see. This is a key aspect of faith—**IT OPERATES IN THE NOW!** Walking by faith means not saying, "sometime later," but recognizing that it is already done in the spiritual realm and bringing that reality into the present moment. This is why the Bible refers to faith as being "in the now." When you walk by faith, you are not traveling linearly through time but vertically, accessing the eternal truth that God has already established.

The Bible tells us to call things that are

not as though they are because they have already been accomplished in the spiritual realm. The devil tries to bring time into the equation to hinder faith. If he can make you focus on time, you can't walk by faith. Faith requires letting go of the constraints of time.

For many years, Christians have struggled to walk in the promises of God due to one problem: **tense.** The Hebrew language does not have a future tense, emphasizing the importance of operating in the *now* kind of faith. When you operate in this faith, you transition from a realm of humanity to divinity. As discussed, when God steps in, He operates outside of time. It's not seedtime and harvest; it's seed and harvest simultaneously. By operating in God's kind of faith, you let go of time constraints, bringing uncommon acceleration into your life. You are not bound by linear time; you are moving vertically, bringing the impossible into your present situation.

Faith in the Now

Faith is powerful and operates in the present. Mark 11:24 states, *"What things soever you desire, when you pray, believe that you receive them, and you shall have them."* This means when you pray for something, such as healing, you must believe you have received it at that moment. This belief is not linear—it's not about waiting for future results. Instead, it involves moving into the spiritual realm where God's promises are already established and imposing them on your current situation.

For example, if you need healing, you don't say, "I will be healed." Instead, you recognize that the Word of God has already declared, *"By His stripes, you were healed."* (I Peter 2:24) You bring this truth into your present reality, believing and declaring out of your mouth that you are healed now, regardless of current symptoms. Similarly, if you need provision, you declare God's promises over your situation immediately. This is true faith—**believing and receiving in the now.**

Power and Authority

Power and authority have been given to you. They are two different words. Power is the capacity to do something. Authority is the position by which you do it. Luke 9:1 states that power and authority were given to the disciples. They exercised this when Peter and John healed a lame man in Acts 3.

We also see in 2 Kings 1:9-11 Elijah operating with authority when the king sent men to capture him and he declared, *"If I be a man of God, then let fire come down from heaven and consume thee and thy fifty."* Elijah's authority came from his faith in God's power. This illustrates the confidence that comes from knowing one's authority in God and can be developed only by faith.

This can even be seen in nature. Imagine a lion in the jungle. Its dominance is not due to its size but its heart. A lion sees every animal, even an elephant, as potential food because it knows it is the king of the jungle. When you have faith in God, you operate in authority. When you walk into a hospital, walk as if you have already been healed. When you walk into your office, walk as if favor has been bestowed upon you. When you experience lack, remember that the wealth of the wicked is stored up for you.

Consider the account of Jesus healing the centurion's servant (Matthew 8:5-13). When the centurion approaches Jesus to request healing for his servant, Jesus offers to go and heal him. However, the centurion asks Jesus to only speak a word and his servant will be healed. In doing so the centurion emphasizes the significance of authority, explaining that when he tells his servant to 'Go,' he obeys, and when he says 'Come,' he comes. Jesus recognizes this understanding and highlights the remarkable faith the centurion possesses. We read in Matthew 8:13 (NKJV), "*And his servant was healed that same hour.*"

This account of Jesus healing the centurion's servant reveals the profound connection between authority and the spoken word. The centurion recognized that Jesus' words carried the power to heal, demonstrating his deep understanding of faith and authority. This encounter illustrates that faith is not just about believing in God's power but also about speaking with authority His promises into existence. Just as Jesus' words brought immediate healing, our words, when spoken in faith, hold the power to transform our circumstances. The centurion's faith in the authority of Jesus' words serves as a powerful reminder that we also have the power and authority to bring the supernatural into the natural world through the words we speak.

Reflections

- Reflect on the level of faith you possess at this moment. Are you fully convinced of God'spromises, or do you find yourself wavering? If your faith is dwindling, ask God to increase it.

- Consider the moment you accepted Christ and were born again. When did it happen? Reflect on that transformative experience and praise God for what He has done in your life.

- Take time to read Hebrews 11. Allow the stories of faith to speak to you in a new way, inspiring and strengthening your own journey of faith.

6

Confession of Faith

---

*"Death and life are in the power of the tongue,
and those who love it will eat its fruit."*

Proverbs 18:21 (NKJV)

Power of Your Words

Kenneth Hagin once said, "Faith is a door to the supernatural." This door has two hinges: believing and speaking. Believing is the first step, and speaking is the crucial next step. Sometimes, if we are not careful, our own words might cancel the promise of God in our lives. Our vocal cords were designed for our victory; our words were designed to create things around us. Many times, it's easy to believe in uncommon acceleration. The speaking part, however, can be more challenging. Whenever a prophecy is released, by faith, we need to **SEE** it, **SAY** it, and **SEIZE** it. In other words, we envision the promise, declare the promise, and seize the promise.

Words hold immense power. John 1:1 states, *"In the beginning was the Word, and the Word was with God."* Among all titles, John describes God as the Word. This Word became flesh, showing that what we articulate can become reality. The Logos word became something tangible. Similarly, the words you speak can become tangible realities.

The wonders God intends to perform in your life are unprecedented. The term 'logos' signifies that words have the potential to become realities. The words you utter can transform into 'things.' In our context, these realities, or 'things,' are significant.

God is ready to perform many significant acts in your life. However, the devil aims to stop these manifestations by targeting your words. He knows that your words will turn into the things God intends to do in your life. Therefore, the articulation of your words is of utmost importance.

Your Words Can Create Or Destroy

Words are like weapons, and you should be trained to use them appropriately. Some of us might think, "I don't speak any bad words, so I'm okay." But look at what the Bible says in Matthew 12:36 *"But I say unto you, that every idle word that men shall speak, they shall give account thereof in the day of judgment."* Every idle word! Every word without purpose!

Sometimes, it may not be bad words but just pointless words. On one side, you are trying to build your faith and plant the promises of God in your heart. On the other side, gossip might be digging a hole to cause destruction.

These days, I often hear people say, "I'm just venting it out." Venting is not a spiritual practice; it's not the fruit of the Spirit. Sometimes, we get so used to making these jokes or comments that we don't realize we are canceling the promises of God in our lives.

Your words can either build up or tear down. Proverbs 18:21 says, *"Death and life are in the power of the tongue: and they that love it shall eat the fruit thereof."* This means that the words you speak have the power to bring life or death. They can create a path for God's promises to manifest, or they can destroy what God is trying to build in your life.

Our words are a tool to release Heaven's purposes on earth. They possess the power to shape your surroundings. Learn to be wise with your words. If you are not careful, you could be canceling the promises God has for you.

Remember, your words are powerful tools given by God to shape your reality. Use them wisely to create the life God has promised you. Be intentional with your speech, and let your words align with the faith you profess. By doing so, you can ensure that your words create rather than destroy, building a foundation for God's promises to come to fruition in your life

Faith vs. Fear

We often think we are speaking faith, but some of us are more fluent in speaking fear. This habit can cancel the promises of God upon our lives.

Sometimes, even when people receive blessing after blessing from God, they respond with doubt and fear. They might think, "Why is everything happening so well? What bad thing is going to come next?" Or they might say, "I'm laughing so much now; that means I'm going to cry soon." God is giving the blessing, God is placing the laughter, and yet we want to cancel it with our words of fear.

For instance, God might use someone to send money to bless you, and you might immediately think, "Why is this person blessing me?" This reaction stems from a mentality accustomed to failure and fear. We become so used to negative words and thoughts that they flow out of us naturally, undermining God's blessings.

God might give you an increase, a promotion, or an opportunity you feel you don't deserve. Instead of embracing it, you might say, "I don't know if I can do this right," or "I don't know if I'm worthy to stand here." These words contradict the promise of God.

Some people are used to famine words or poverty mentality. Even when trained to speak about prosperity, they might revert to old habits around their friends. They might say things like, "Let's go to this reception so we can save money on dinner," joking about not having enough, while forgetting that the same mouth confessed Jehovah Jireh, our provider, in the morning worship.

These jokes might seem harmless, but they reveal a deeper issue. They show how easily we can bow to the spirit of lack and fear, even after professing faith. Feelings and emotions matter, but they shouldn't rule us. Added to this is the influence of friends or associations that the enemy uses to cuddle those negative emotions, reinforcing fear and doubt. We often don't pay attention to how our words impact our lives. If you check your words from the morning, you might find that you have already spoken fear or doubt. You might say, "I confessed acceleration in church, but then I joked with my friend. Will that cancel God's big promise in my life?"

The answer lies in understanding the power of your words. Words of fear can indeed undermine the promises of God if we let them. To speak faith consistently, we must train ourselves to reject words of fear and embrace the language of faith.

Faith and fear cannot coexist. When you choose to speak faith, you align yourself with God's promises. When you speak fear, you align yourself with doubt and negativity. Therefore, be vigilant about your words. Let them reflect the faith you profess, and watch as God's promises unfold in your life.

In this journey of faith, your words play a crucial role. They can create or destroy. Choose to speak faith, reject fear, and embrace the blessings that God has in store for you.

Faith is the Language of Heaven

For most of us, our original language or mother tongue is familiar and easy to use. However, if you travel to another country and speak in your native language, say Telugu, the people there may not understand you. You would need a translator to communicate. This is similar to what happens between Earth and Heaven. The language of Heaven is Faith, but we often speak in the language of worry and fear. Heaven does not understand this language.

This disconnect is why much of the Earth remains as it is, instead of reflecting Heaven. We need more people on this Earth whose language matches that of Heaven. Let me illustrate this with an example.

God created the world with a seen world and an unseen world. Just because it is unseen doesn't mean it doesn't exist. All that we see belongs to the seen world, while all the promises of God belong to the unseen world. God exists in both realms. Ephesians 1:3 says, *"Blessed be the God and Father of our Lord Jesus Christ, who has blessed us with all spiritual blessings in heavenly places."* These blessings are in the unseen world.

According to II Peter 1:3, all things pertaining to life and godliness have been given to us. So, all the things we need are in the unseen world. We are here in the seen world, asking Heaven to deliver the answers to our prayers.

Some of you might be praying for God's blessings in your life, saying, "Lord, bless me." God's desire is to bless you. Think about how you order something on Amazon. When they deliver it, they ask for a code—your pin code or OTP. If the code matches, the delivery is made.

Similarly, blessings come from Heaven. For the blessings to be delivered, the code in the unseen world is "blessed," but if you keep saying "bless me," the code doesn't match, and the blessing cannot be delivered.

If you need healing and you keep asking, "Heal me," while Heaven's language says "healed," the codes don't match. You might be praying, fasting, and doing everything right, but without the correct language, the healing is not delivered. Open your Bible, find the right passcode, and give the OTP to the angels, and they will deliver it.

Instead of saying, "God, heal me," declare, "I am healed." It doesn't matter if your body is hurting or if you have multiple reports from the doctor. You need to say, "I am healed," and then the language matches, and Heaven will deliver. This is how we draw from the invisible to the visible, and this is how manifestation takes place from the unseen to the seen.

Many people want to be used in God's kingdom and pray, "God, what is my calling?" But Heaven says, "You are called to leave a mark on this planet." You need to start declaring, "I am called; I have a calling upon my life." When you know the power of your words and change your language, you will see God's blessings manifest from the unseen world to the seen world.

Heaven is anticipating God's children to speak in its language. Sadly, for some, packages remain undelivered. After salvation, the moment you are saved in the seen world, angels are ready with your packages. Salvation is a package that includes not just forgiveness of sins but also healing, wholeness, and deliverance. The entire package is waiting in Heaven to be delivered to you. You simply have to claim it!

What we have that others don't is the revelation from Matthew 13:10-11. The disciples asked Jesus why He spoke in parables. He answered, *"Because it is given unto you to know the mysteries of the kingdom of heaven, but to them, it is not given."* The mysteries of Heaven are revealed to you, and the enemy tries to cover the truth. But through the revelation of God's Word, these mysteries are being opened for you.

Wisdom from Proverbs

Proverbs 15:1 (ESV) says, "*A soft word turns away wrath, but a harsh word stirs up anger.*" Wise people learn from others' experiences; some learn only from their own experience; fools never learn.

Proverbs 11:9 (KJV) says, "*A hypocrite with his mouth destroyeth his neighbor: but through knowledge shall the just be delivered.*" As clearly inferred from the proverb, there is no vaccine for trouble. God doesn't shield the righteous from trouble but He does deliver them out of it.

Proverbs 15:4 (ESV) states, "*A gentle tongue is a tree of life, but perverseness in it breaks the spirit.*" A family where all the members speak gently, or a church where people speak kindly, or an office where everyone converses politely is like a Garden of Paradise where one would want to live forever.

Proverbs 16:24 (NLT) declares, "*Kind words are like honey—sweet to the soul and healthy for the body.*"

All of the verses from the previous page emphasize the importance of the words we speak.

Reflections

- "A gentle tongue is a tree of life..." Proverbs 15:4 (ESV). Reflect on this scripture.

- Take a few moments to reflect on what you have been saying from the time you woke up this morning until now. Consider how your words shaped your day.

- "Venting is not a spiritual practice. It is not the fruit of the Spirit."

- Observe what you say to others when you express your hurt, anger, or disappointment. Pray that the Lord will fill you with self-control and peace.

7

Hold Fast to Your Confession

---

*"Since then we have a great high priest who has passed
through the heavens, Jesus, the Son of God,
let us hold fast our confession."*

Hebrews 4:14 (ESV)

The Power of Confession

You might have heard discussions about positive thinking or positive confessions. There's something we need to understand regarding confession. What is confession according to the Word of God? In Greek, it's called homologia, which means *to say the same thing* or *to agree*. Confession is saying the same things as the Word of God or agreeing with the Word of God.

Anytime you don't agree or speak contrary to the Word, you are confessing against the Word of God.

Hebrews 4:14 says, *"Seeing then that we have a great high priest that is passed into the heavens, Jesus the Son of God, let us hold fast our confession."* The scripture instructs us to hold fast. According to the Greek translation, this means to master something—to become very good at it. We know how to confess; we speak here and there, we confess in church, we confess in our prayers. But the Bible is talking about holding fast to your confession. Hebrews 2:1 says, *"Therefore we ought to give the more earnest heed to the things which we have heard, lest at any time we should let them slip."* The problem is that we are confessing, but sometimes we don't hold fast. Sometimes things just slip away.

Filling yourself with the Word (the water), and confessing God's promises is like filling water into a bottle. However, if that bottle has even a minute hole in the bottom, drop by drop, that water will leak out. This is what happens with our confessions. In this season of acceleration, we may think we are confessing and holding fast to our confession. But some jokes with friends, some casual conversations, some gossip—as Matthew says, idle words—cause the Word to slip away. If this keeps happening, we won't see the promises of God manifesting in our lives.

We must ensure that our words always align with God's Word. This is not just a casual practice but a disciplined and consistent effort. When you truly hold fast to your confession, you are continually agreeing with what God has said, regardless of circumstances. This unwavering confession is the key to seeing God's promises manifest in your life.

The Example of Jesus and Abraham

Jesus, our role model, consistently held fast to His confession. Hebrews 3:1 declares Jesus as the Apostle and High Priest of our profession. This means, He has already walked the path before us and was a master at it. As we continue to read that chapter, we will see that Jesus faced temptations in every way! He would have also been tempted to let go of His confession.

There were many instances where He was pressured to the extreme, and it would have been easy to let His confession slip. But the Word says that, despite being tempted, He never uttered a word that was contrary to His father's will. He remained faithful, even unto death.

Let us suppose you have a fever. If you are not careful, the pattern of your confessions might look something like this:

DAY 1 ⇒ You boldly say, "By His stripes, I am healed."

DAY 2 ⇒ You declare, "I receive divine health into my body."

DAY 3 ⇒ The temperature doesn't seem to be coming down, yet you confess, "Healing is my portion."

DAY 4 ⇒ You remain silent.

DAY 5 ⇒ You say "I think I have dengue."

What has happened in this example? The enemy has pushed you to a point where you allow your confession to slip. Matthew 12:37 (KJV) says, "*For by thy words thou shalt be justified, and by thy words thou shalt be condemned.*" This means that we will be judged based on our words. It also means that when we speak contrary to the Word of God, it can open a door for the enemy to enter our lives. How careful should we be with our confessions! Every word matters and every confession counts.

Words as Fruits, Not Seeds

When we talk about your confession or your words, many interpret these words as seeds. However, in the spiritual realm, words are not seeds but fruits. Proverbs 18:21 says, *"Death and life are in the power of the tongue: and they that love it shall eat the fruit thereof."* Your words are fruits.

How does this fruit come about? Every fruit comes from a seed, and the seeds are the voices sown in your heart. Everything you listen to, everything you read, everything you hear from people you are connected to—these are seeds being sown into your heart. From your mouth, the fruit comes out.

Hebrews 13:15 says, *"By him therefore let us offer the sacrifice of praise to God continually, that is, the fruit of our lips giving thanks to his name."* So when I say words are fruits, I mean they are the end result. In other words, when you say that you are healed, you are claiming the end result; you are claiming the fruit.

What you talk about constantly is very important. The seeds are sown continuously, and the fruits are ripened continuously. In this process, you need to hold fast to your confession. Ensure that your words, which are the fruits, align with the seeds of faith sown in your heart. This consistency will lead to the manifestation of God's promises in your life.

Acting on Your Confession

James 2:26 says, *"Faith without works is dead."* This means that our faith must be accompanied by corresponding actions to be alive and effective.

Consider the testimony of a lady who is part of our church family and claimed God's promises for her. The word of uncommon acceleration was sown into the heart of this lady and she believed that she would conceive. She and her husband confessed this word and followed it with a corresponding obedient action. How did she prove her faith? By taking the pregnancy test first thing in the morning. And God rewarded her faith, because her pregnancy test came positive!

Her action demonstrated her belief in the word she had received. So, for all of us who are confessing uncommon acceleration, what do our actions look like in the areas where we are believing for acceleration? Take time to reflect on your actions. Are they aligning with the confessions you make?

Let us look at a Biblical example. In Mark 11:12-25 we read of Jesus cursing the fig tree. In that story, the results were evident within 24 hours. After Jesus cursed the fig tree, He didn't go back to check on it or speak about it again. It was His disciples who noticed the withered tree. This shows that Jesus spoke the word and acted with faith, without doubting.

Also, consider the life of Abraham. He held fast to his confession for more than 24 years before he saw the promise fulfilled. He did not waver in his faith but demonstrated corresponding actions throughout his journey.

It is important to understand that you will receive the promise of God according to your faith. But your actions must reflect your faith. If you are believing for uncommon acceleration, your actions should show it. Don't just speak the words; act on them with unwavering faith.

Holding fast to your confession means not letting any doubt or idle words slip in. It means aligning your actions with your words consistently. Whether the manifestation comes in 24 hours or 24 years, your faith, coupled with corresponding actions, will bring God's promises to fruition in your life.

Embracing Uncommon Acceleration

As you meditate on these words, you will receive the revelation knowledge that God has shined forth onto you through His Word. I pray that you experience Uncommon Acceleration in every aspect of your life; and that your life becomes a living testimony of God's grace, goodness and love for you.

In the journey we have taken together through the pages of this book, we have learned that faith is not merely about believing and speaking, but also, about mastering the art of holding onto our confessions, even in the face of challenges and doubts. Our words have the power to shape our reality. When coupled with unwavering faith and intentional actions, they bring about extraordinary acceleration and transformation in every aspect of our lives.

From the silent growth of the bamboo tree to the unwavering faith of Abraham and the authoritative declarations of Jesus, we have witnessed the transformative potential that lies within us when we align our words with faith and act intentionally.

Just as the bamboo tree's roots grow silently underground before it shoots up toward the sky, our faith often begins as a seed planted deep within our hearts. We can nurture our faith by listening to God's Word, staying firm in our beliefs, and putting God first in everything. By doing this, we can achieve amazing things, just like the bamboo tree that seemed unlikely to reach great heights.

It is time to bring our story full circle as

we conclude our journey of comprehending what Uncommon Acceleration is. Just as the bamboo tree eventually emerges from its silent phase to tower over the landscape and as Abraham's faith led to the fulfillment of God's promises, it is time for us to step into the fullness of our potential and embrace the abundant blessings that await us.

So, let us resolve to continue nurturing our faith, holding fast to our confessions, and carrying out intentional actions that align with the promises of God. As we do, may our lives become living testimonies of God's grace, goodness, and love, shining brightly for all to see. And just like the bamboo tree that reaches towering heights, may we also rise to new levels of faith and experience the extraordinary acceleration that comes from walking in alignment with God's Word.

With hearts full of gratitude and

anticipation, let us move forward into the abundant future that awaits us, knowing that 'with God, all things are possible'.

Reflections

- Pray fervently towards walking in alignment with God's Word and ask the Holy Spirit to help you.

- Cancel every curse spoken over you or your family. Renounce any activity or confession that undermines your faith.

- Journal the significant and God-breathed moments you experienced while reading this book and living out the Uncommon Acceleration in your walk with God.

8

Testimonies of Uncommon Acceleration

My Journey to Hair Restoration

I experienced extreme hair fall. My son noticed it and expressed concern as well. I encouraged him to thank God with me for every strand of hair lost, believing that it would be replaced with the strongest strands.

During the 21 days of fasting and prayer, I tuned into the live telecast from home at the dining table. At one point, Ps. Arpitha released a blessing for everyone experiencing hair fall. My son and I exchanged joyful glances, as we both recognized the significance of the word delivered. Immediately, in the week that followed, my hair fall was reduced to a minimum. Thank you, Pastor Arpitha, for considering our needs and praying for us!

I have experienced uncommon acceleration in both health and joy. All glory to God for providing us with more than we ask, exceedingly and abundantly!

Malvika Reddy

Healing from Psoriasis

I suffered from psoriasis for twenty years. I had very thick layers of scales on my scalp, which made my head feel extremely heavy. This condition eventually spread to my body as well. I visited many hospitals and tried various treatments for homeopathic, Ayurvedic, and allopathic but everyone told me that psoriasis had no cure. I endured a lot because of this.

During the January 2023 Fasting Prayers, as Pastor Ben preached on Luke 10:17-19, I received a revelation from the Word of God. I felt as if psoriasis fell away like lightning from heaven, and I was no longer afflicted by it. I believed with all my heart that, by His stripes, I was already healed.

After hearing about Uncommon Acceleration, I embraced and meditated on this promise. By June, I experienced the manifestation of this promise. One morning, I woke up to find that the scales had completely disappeared from my head, and I was entirely free from psoriasis. It was as though my healing had happened as quickly as bamboo shoots grow.

This is the miraculous work of God in my life, and I praise Him for this uncommon acceleration in my healing. I have been delivered from the sickness that oppressed me for 20 years through the Word of God. I give glory to God and thank the Pastors for teaching us to trust in His Word.

Vijaya

From Struggle to Abundance

Over the past three years, my wife and I have witnessed an uncommon acceleration in our lives as we gained a deeper understanding of our identity in Christ Jesus. Previously, we struggled to make ends meet, barely covering our home loan EMI with no money left over by the month's end. However, as we delved into the Word of God through our pastors' teachings on Jesus' finished work and divine plans for our lives, we began to prioritize seeking God's Kingdom. Consequently, all aspects of our lives fell into place without us having to chase after them.

I had been stuck in a stagnant job for 16 years, while my wife was in a similar situation for 6 years. But in a remarkably short period, I received a promotion from manager to director, accompanied by substantial hikes and bonuses twice a year—a rarity in our company. I also started traveling internationally for work.

My wife also experienced rapid recognition at her workplace, receiving 16 awards in just one year. Additionally, God blessed us with two new cars. Through this uncommon acceleration, we are now able to sow more than ever before into God's Kingdom, living out our calling to be a blessing to others.

Pradeep

Divine Provision in a Time of Crisis

My younger daughter works in the US. In May, she encountered a problem with her visa, and her job contract came to an end. Since she lives alone there and had recently purchased a new car, she needed to pay the car EMIs. Everything seemed upside down. If she didn't secure another job, she would either have to return to India or pursue higher studies, which was financially unviable.

At that time, I attended the fasting prayers at New City Church, where Pastor Arpitha released a word about uncommon acceleration. I held on to the word and declared uncommon acceleration in my daughter's situation. As I prayed for a swift resolution to the crisis we found ourselves in, we continued to believe in uncommon acceleration.

Remarkably, within the same month of the release of the word, my daughter was offered two different jobs, both without requiring an interview process. She had the option to choose between them. All glory to God. I thank our pastors for the anointed word of God.

Ramani

From Dream to Reality of Owning a Home

It was my dream to buy a house in Hyderabad. I had been trying for the past few years, but nothing seemed to work. When the word about 'uncommon acceleration' was released, I believed that God could make things happen quickly in my situation. I began confessing the word every day.

I held on to the word and trusted that it would manifest regarding my house. Within two months, a person approached us with an offer for an apartment that suited our needs. Although I was unfamiliar with the entire process, God's favor and acceleration made it possible for us to become owners of a new apartment. It was indeed an uncommon acceleration, and suddenly everything fell into place.

I received my house documents in no time. I am the first person in my family to buy a new house. One of my cousins, who does not know Jesus, testified that "The LORD you serve made it possible." I thank God and our pastors for encouraging us to trust in the word of God.

Sarika

Responding to Christ

"If you openly declare that Jesus is Lord and believe in your heart that God raised him from the dead, you will be saved. For it is by believing in your heart that you are made right with God, and it is by openly declaring your faith that you are saved...For whosoever shall call upon the name of the Lord shall be saved."
Romans 10:9-10,13

As you have read this book, I believe your spirit has been stirred. The best decision of your life is to receive and accept Jesus Christ as your Lord and personal Savior. It is the most important decision you'll ever make!

By His grace, God has already done everything to provide salvation. You simply believe and receive it.

Pray Aloud:

"Jesus, I confess that You are my Lord and Savior. I believe in my heart that God raised You from the dead. By faith in Your written Word, I receive my salvation now. Thank You, Jesus, for saving me."

The very moment you commit your life to Jesus Christ, the truth of His Word instantly comes to pass in your spirit. You are a brand-new creation. A species that never existed before.

Receiving the Holy Spirit

"For everyone who asks, receives. Everyone who seeks, finds.
And to everyone who knocks, the door will be opened....
how much more will your heavenly Father give the
Holy Spirit to those who ask him."

Luke 11:10-13

As His child, your loving heavenly Father desires to give you the supernatural power needed to live this new life. All you need to do is ask, believe, and receive!

Pray Aloud:

"Father, I recognize my need for Your power to live this new life. Please fill me with Your Holy Spirit. By faith, I receive it right now. Thank You for

baptizing me. Holy Spirit, You are welcome in my life." **Congratulations—you are now filled with God's supernatural power!**

Some syllables from a language you don't recognize will rise up from your heart to your mouth (1 Cor 14:14). As you speak them out loud by faith, you are releasing God's power from within and building yourself up in the spirit (1 Cor. 14:4). You can do this whenever and wherever you like.

It doesn't really matter whether you felt anything or not when you prayed to receive the Lord and His Holy Spirit. If you believed in your heart that you received, then God's Word promises you did. *"Therefore I say to you, whatever things you ask when you pray, believe that you receive them, and you will have them."* (Mark 11:24) **God always honors His Word—believe it!**

Please contact us and let us know if you have received Jesus as your savior or have been baptized with the Holy Spirit. We would love to celebrate with you and help you better understand what has taken place in your life. You can check out our book **'I'm Saved! What's Next?'** to help you grow in your new relationship with God.

Notes

Notes

Notes

Notes

8AM — ENGLISH SERVICE — LIVE STREAM

10:30AM — TELUGU SERVICE — LIVE STREAM / CALVARY TV

SANDHYA CONVENTION, GACHIBOWLI, HYDERABAD

90106 43687   info@newcity.in

NEW CITY CHURCH ORIGINALS:

I'M SAVED! WHAT'S NEXT!
By Pastor Benjamin Komanapalli Jr.

UNCOMMON ACCELERATION
By Dr. Arpitha Komanapalli

AUTHORITY OF THE BELIEVER
By Pastor Benjamin Komanapalli Jr.